INSTANT
Independent Reading
Response Activities

by Laura Witmer

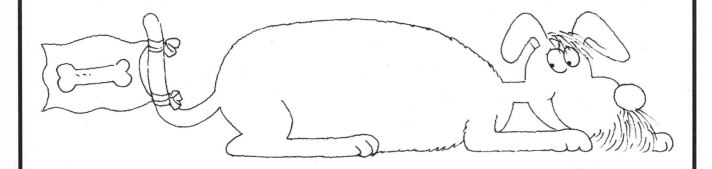

SCHOLASTIC
PROFESSIONAL BOOKS

New York ♦ Toronto ♦ London ♦ Auckland ♦ Sydney ♦ Mexico City ♦ New Delhi ♦ Hong Kong ♦ Buenos Aires

To my family—
Thank you for your patience and support.

Cover design Josué Castilleja
Cover illustrations by Tammie Lyon

Interior design by Ellen Matlach Hassell
for Boultinghouse & Boultinghouse, Inc.

Interior illustrations by Paul Harvey

ISBN: 0-439-30961-1

Contents

Independent Reading Projects

Introduction

Welcome to *Instant Independent Reading Response Activities*—a flexible and easy-to-use collection of quick reading response projects that can be used with any book. Whether you are looking for a complete independent reading program or activities to supplement your existing program, this book offers something for everyone. Kids will enjoy responding to their independent reading books with 50 activities that reinforce the key story elements that second through fourth graders need to know: characters, setting, problem and resolution, sequence of events, and more.

Everything in this book is designed for children to use instantly and independently. Each activity includes a reproducible sheet that shows kids exactly what to do with easy, step-by-step directions, a short list of materials, and an example of a completed project. Most projects include a reproducible activity sheet as well. You'll also find rubrics, a checklist, a reading log, a conference form, and other materials that will help both you and your students stay organized throughout the year. The section titled "How to Use This Book" takes you through each step of implementing an effective independent reading program, from organizing your classroom library to assessing students' work.

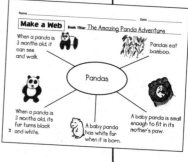

The reading program that I've developed allows students to take responsibility and ownership of their independent reading. Students are encouraged to make their own choices throughout the process. They learn to select appropriate reading materials, choose the project they wish to complete, and evaluate their own work with a self-assessment rubric. To stay organized, children keep all of their materials in an independent reading folder. These folders also allow the teacher to keep track of students' work and share their progress with families.

When students take responsibility for their independent reading, they become more enthusiastic readers. And the more children read and respond to literature, the stronger their reading skills will become. I have used these activities with students of all reading levels and have found that even my most reluctant readers enjoy working on them. Students can complete the activities with any book and at their own pace. This allows children to feel confident and positive about the process. I know that my students are on the road to becoming better readers when I hear them ask, "Can I work on my independent reading folder?"

How to Use This Book

The activities in this book can be used as a complete independent reading program or they can supplement your existing program. You might adapt activities or choose those that best meet the needs of your students. In addition to the 50 activities, you'll find rubrics, a checklist, a reading log, and other helpful materials. This section walks you through the management system that I use to help my students stay motivated, organized, and on task. You'll find strategies for organizing a classroom library, helping students choose appropriate reading materials, assessing students' work, and much more.

Organizing Your Classroom Library

To help students choose books of the appropriate reading level, I level the books in my classroom library by labeling them with red, yellow, and blue dot stickers (found in any office supply store). To make it even easier for students to locate books of a particular level, I store the books by level in red, yellow, and blue plastic containers. This also helps students return books to the correct location. Suggested guidelines for each level are as follows:

Red Level
- repetitive, easy-to-read text
- simple sentence structure
- appropriate for lower grades

Yellow Level
- no repetition in text
- more complicated sentence structure
- appropriate for present grade level

Blue Level
- more complicated sentence structure
- more text per page
- includes chapters
- appropriate for next grade level

Organizing Supplies

Make copies of the activity sheets and directions sheets for each project. Store them in hanging file folders in a plastic crate. Label each hanging folder with the project name and number, and file them in numerical order. Ask students to tell you if they take the last copy in a folder. (To cut down on photocopying, glue each directions sheet to construction paper. Laminate them for even greater durability. Store these sheets in the appropriate file folders and ask students to return them when they are finished. You might make two or three copies so that several students can work on the same activity at one time.)

Store other supplies nearby in a separate plastic crate. This helps students find what they need easily and independently. The following supplies are needed for the projects in the book:

- construction paper
- markers, crayons, and pencils
- hole punch
- index cards
- colored sentence strip paper
- paper plates

- craft sticks and straws
- magazines
- yarn
- plastic and paper bags
- scissors
- glue, tape, and stapler

Helping Students Choose Books

Teach students how to select a book that matches their reading level and interests. Encourage children to read the first few pages of a book to determine if the subject interests them. Let them know that they can always return a book and choose a different one if they feel they didn't make a good selection.

Here are two "tests" to help children determine if a book is at the appropriate reading level for them:

1. Hold your hand in a fist. Open to the middle of the book and read one page. Each time you come to a word you do not know, put up one finger. When you have finished reading one page, look at how many fingers are up. If all five fingers are up, the book is probably too difficult.

2. Have older students ask themselves questions about the book. If they answer "yes" to the following questions, the book is probably the right level.
   - Do you know most of the words?
   - Are you able to figure out most of the words you don't know?
   - Do you understand most of the ideas?

Introducing the Process

There are several steps involved in using the independent reading projects in this book. To introduce the process, work through each step once together using a book you have read together as a class. With practice and guidance, children should soon be able to move through the process independently.

The following steps are described in greater detail throughout this section.

1. Children choose a book.

2. Children make a prediction about their book in their reading response journal.

3. Children read to themselves, to a classmate, and to a parent or another adult at home.

4. In their reading response journals, children write responses to questions posted by the teacher.

5. When they are finished with their book, children write a response in their reading response journal.

6. Children choose and complete a project from the project checklist. (You might have children complete more than one project or you might specify the project for children to complete.)

7. Children evaluate their work using a self-assessment rubric.

8. Children schedule a teacher conference.

> ### Tip
> Work with students to set guidelines for behavior so that independent reading time is productive. Post the guidelines in your room and remind students of them before you start the period. If problems arise, encourage students to help you come up with a resolution.

Introducing the Independent Reading Folders

To help students organize their materials, provide each of them with a two-pocket folder. Show students each of the materials in the folder and explain its purpose as described below. In the folder, students store the following materials:

- ♦ project list
- ♦ checklist
- ♦ reading log
- ♦ reading response journal
- ♦ their current independent reading book
- ♦ completed projects or works in progress for their current book
- ♦ self-assessment rubric

Project List

This two-page sheet lists all 50 activities in this book. Students use the list to choose one or more projects to complete for each book they read. On the project list, students record the date they completed the project and the title of the book on which the project was based. Although it is acceptable for students to complete the same project for different books, it is a good idea to encourage children to try new projects. This list allows children to keep track of which projects they have completed and provides the teacher with a quick reference to check children's progress. Children will need new lists throughout the year.

Checklist

The checklist helps students stay organized throughout the entire process. If students are not sure of what to do next, they can refer to their checklist. On the checklist, students fill in their name, the book title, author, and reading level. When students have completed a step, they check the box beside that step. After students have read to a classmate and family member, they ask the listener to sign their checklist. This builds students' sense of responsibility and also encourages families to be involved in their children's independent reading.

Reading Log

On the reading log, students keep a record of all of the books they read during the year. Each time a student reads a book, he or she records the title, author, and level of the book. This is a good reference for both the student and the teacher and is helpful to share with parents at conferences or as needed.

Reading Response Journal

The purpose of the reading response journal is to develop a dialogue about literature between the student and teacher. Provide students with lined blue books or other journals and explain that this is where students will write their ideas and questions about the books they are reading. Periodically collect the journals and respond to what students have written. Encourage them to write even more by asking them questions about what they have written. Encourage children to support their ideas with proof from the book. This provides excellent practice for state competency tests.

After a student has chosen a book, the student writes the book title and author in his or her journal. The student then makes a prediction about what the book will be about based on the book's cover. When students have finished a book, they write why they did or did not like the book. You might also have students record words from their book that they do not know along with definitions.

To encourage students to write even more in their journals, write a question on the board each day or week. (You might write more than one question and have students choose which one to answer.) Have students record the question and the date and then respond to the question in writing. (Remind students that they should always

explain their answer and provide examples from the book for support.) Here are some suggested journal questions:

- ♦ Do you think the illustrations match the story? Why or why not?
- ♦ Were any parts of the book funny? What made them funny?
- ♦ What do you find most challenging about your book? Why?
- ♦ Do you think the characters are believable? Why or why not?
- ♦ Do you think the main character made good decisions? Why or why not?
- ♦ Would you change anything about the book? What would you change and why?
- ♦ How do you think the book will end? Why do you think it will end this way?
- ♦ Write a letter to a character in the book. Include questions for the character to answer.
- ♦ What do you think was the most important event in the book so far? Why?
- ♦ Did the beginning of the book make you want to keep reading? Why or why not?

> ## Tip
>
> To build students' speaking skills, give them the opportunity to share their completed projects with another student or with the class. You may want to set aside a separate time for sharing so the noise level does not interfere with independent reading time. Remind children not to give away the ending of their books when they are sharing their projects with one another.

Assessing Student Work

It is a good idea to involve children in the assessment process. Have students evaluate their own work by filling in the rubric on page 15. I also have found it helpful to have brief conferences with individual students to assess their comprehension of each book.

Self-Assessment Rubric

Show students how to fill in the self-assessment rubric. Explain that if a project does not have a writing or art component, students can leave that section blank. Tell students that they can make corrections in their work if they feel it is necessary. The self-assessment process encourages children to check that they have finished all the steps and also builds an awareness of the areas they can work on for the next project.

Teacher Rubric

This more detailed rubric provides a quick way for the teacher to evaluate each student's work. Again, leave sections blank if they do not apply to a particular project.

Conference Form

When students are finished with a project and have completed a self-assessment rubric, have them sign up for a teacher conference. (Hang a clipboard near your desk where students can write their names.) The conference form provides a guide for the conference and includes two areas for the teacher to evaluate: the student's ability to retell parts of the story and the student's reading fluency. Meeting with students also allows the teacher to determine if students are choosing appropriate reading materials.

Ask students to retell or describe various story elements: sequence of events, problem and resolution, characters, setting, and so on. These are listed on the conference sheet. Check the column that describes the student's retelling of a particular story element: detailed, partial, or incomplete. You can choose a few of the story elements for students to retell at each conference.

Next, ask students questions about the book and encourage them to provide reasons for their answers. For at least one question, have students find and read aloud a passage in the book to support their answer. This allows the teacher to assess reading fluency. Check the column that best describes how students sound out unfamiliar words, pay attention to punctuation, read with expression, and so on. Here are some examples of conference questions:

- ◆ Why did you choose this book?
- ◆ Is this a fiction or nonfiction book? How can you tell?
- ◆ What was your favorite part? Why?
- ◆ How did the main character feel at the beginning and the end of the book?
- ◆ Do you think the setting was good for the book? Why or why not?
- ◆ How would you describe the main character?
- ◆ What was the problem?
- ◆ How was the problem solved?
- ◆ What happened at the beginning, middle, and end of the story?
- ◆ What did you learn from this book?
- ◆ Did you like the book? Why or why not?

> ## Tip
> Display students' completed projects in the hallway or in the classroom to show what students are reading.

Project List

		Book Title	Date Completed
1	Book Cover		
2	Favorite Part		
3	Bookmark		
4	Word Cards		
5	Picture Mural		
6	Word Graph		
7	Make a Web		
8	Create a New Page		
9	Story Sequence		
10	Opposites		
11	Likes/Dislikes		
12	Make a Puzzle		
13	Scrambled Sentences		
14	Paper-Bag Puppet		
15	Paper-Plate Puppet		
16	Stick Puppet		
17	Advertise-a-Book Poster		
18	Sentence Sequence Chart		
19	Story Flip Book		
20	Character Map		
21	Book Award		
22	Adjective Fan		
23	Story Questions		
24	New Ending		
25	Story Chart		

Instant Independent Reading Response Activities   Scholastic Professional Books

Name _____ Date _____

Project List

	Book Title	Date Completed
26 Story Map		
27 Picture Walk		
28 Pyramid Diorama		
29 Postcard		
30 Story Flag		
31 Letter to the Author		
32 Story Cube		
33 Character Feeling Chart		
34 Mirror, Mirror		
35 Noun Flip Book		
36 Rhyming Chain		
37 Real or Make-Believe?		
38 Character Venn Diagram		
39 Fact Finder		
40 True or False?		
41 Cause and Effect		
42 Just the Facts		
43 Facts and Opinions		
44 Event Timeline		
45 Story Booklet		
46 Setting Map		
47 Story Quilt Square		
48 Book Banner		
49 Create a Poem		
50 Book News		

Instant Independent Reading Response Activities Scholastic Professional Books

Name _____ Date _____

Checklist

Book Title: _____

Author: _____

Reading Level: _____

☐ **1.** I wrote a prediction in my reading response journal.

☐ **2.** I filled in my reading log.

☐ **3.** I read the book myself.

☐ **4.** I read the book to a classmate. _____
signature

☐ **5.** I read the book to an adult at home. _____
signature

☐ **6.** I finished reading my book.

☐ **7.** I completed a project and filled in the project list.

☐ **8.** I answered a question in my reading response journal.

☐ **9.** I wrote why I did or did not like my book in my reading response journal.

☐ **10.** I filled in a self-assessment rubric.

☐ **11.** I scheduled a conference with my teacher.

☐ **12.** I'm ready to choose a new book!

Reading Log

Name _____

Date	Book Title	Author	Level

Instant Independent Reading Response Activities Scholastic Professional Books

Name _____ Date _____

Self-Assessment Rubric

Book Title: _____

Author: _____

Reading Level: _____

Project Number and Name: _____

	3 Points	**2 Points**	**1 Point**	**Score**
Directions	I followed all of the directions.	I followed most of the directions.	I did not follow most of the directions.	
Writing	My writing is neat and accurate.	Some of my writing is neat and accurate.	Most of my writing is not neat and accurate.	
Pictures	My pictures illustrate my writing.	My pictures illustrate some of my writing.	My pictures do not illustrate my writing.	

Total Score _____

Instant Independent Reading Response Activities   Scholastic Professional Books

Assessment Rubric

Name _____ Date _____

Book Title _____ Level _____

Components	Characteristics	Ratings					
Title and Author	Legible; neat	1	2	3	4	5	6
	Correct spelling	1	2	3	4	5	6
Directions	Followed directions	1	2	3	4	5	6
Writing	Thoughtful content	1	2	3	4	5	6
	Legible; neat	1	2	3	4	5	6
	Appropriate placement	1	2	3	4	5	6
	Correct spelling	1	2	3	4	5	6
Pictures/Graphics	Follow a logical sequence	1	2	3	4	5	6
	Clear; visible	1	2	3	4	5	6
	Related to theme	1	2	3	4	5	6
	Show sufficient detail	1	2	3	4	5	6
	Colorful	1	2	3	4	5	6
	Neat	1	2	3	4	5	6
Project Total:							

Ratings Key   **1** Incomplete   **2** Needs Improvement   **3** Fair   **4** Emerging   **5** Good   **6** Excellent

Comments

_____

_____

_____

_____

Instant Independent Reading Response Activities Scholastic Professional Books

Conference Form

Name _____ Date _____

Book Title _____ Level _____

Retelling/Describing

Story Element	Detailed	Partial	Incomplete
Beginning			
Setting			
Characters			
Problem			
Sequence of events			
Resolution			

Comments _____

Read Aloud

Skill	Often	Sometimes	Seldom
Self-corrects unfamiliar words			
Sounds out unfamiliar words			
Pays attention to punctuation			
Reads smoothly			
Reads with expression			
Finds appropriate passages			

Comments _____

Professional References

Cochran, Judith. *Everything You Need to Know to Be a Successful Whole Language Teacher: Plans, Strategies, Techniques, and More.* Nashville, Tennessee: Incentive Publications, 1993.

Jackson, Norma R., and Paula L. Pillow. *The Reading-Writing Workshop: Getting Started.* New York: Scholastic Professional Books, 1992.

Karnes, Frances A., and Kristin R. Stephens. *The Ultimate Guide for Student Product Development & Evaluation.* Waco, Texas: Prufrock Press, 1999.

O'Brien-Palmer, Michelle. *Book-Talk.* Kirkland, Washington: MicNik Publications, 1993.

O'Brien-Palmer, Michelle. *Read and Write: Fun Literature and Writing Connections for Kids.* Kirkland, Washington: MicNik Publications, 1994.

Ohlhausen, Marilyn M., and Mary Jepsen. "Lessons from Goldilocks: 'Somebody's Been Choosing My Books But I Can Make My Own Choices Now!'" *The New Advocate,* Vol. 5, No. 1, Winter 1992, p. 36. Norwood, Massachusetts: Christopher-Gordon.

Routman, Regie. *Invitations: Changing as Teachers and Learners K–3.* Portsmouth, New Hampshire: Heinemann, 1991.

Taberski, Sharon. *On Solid Ground: Strategies for Teaching Reading K–3.* Portsmouth, New Hampshire. Heinemann, 2000.

Name _____ Date _____

Book Cover

Materials

✔ your book
✔ plain white paper
✔ pencil
✔ crayons or markers

Steps:

1. Fold the paper in half so that it looks like a book cover.

2. On the front, write the title and author.

3. Under the title and author, draw a picture of a scene from the book.

4. Inside, write a sentence that tells one thing you learned from the book.

5. Draw a picture to illustrate what you learned.

Book Cover Example

Miss Rumphius
by Barbara Cooney

I learned that people can do things to make the world more beautiful, like plant lots of flowers.

Name _____ Date _____

PROJECT 2
Favorite Part

Materials
- ✔ your book
- ✔ Favorite Part sheet
- ✔ crayons or markers
- ✔ pencil

Steps:

1. Draw a picture of your favorite part of the book.

2. Write a few sentences describing your favorite part.

3. Write a few sentences telling why this was your favorite part.

Favorite Part Example

Name _____ Date _____

Favorite Part

Book Title: The Case of the Cat's Meow

This is a picture of my favorite part.

My favorite part of the book was when the boys are camping outside and their alarm clock rings. When they finally turn on their flashlight, they find their friend Snitch.

This was my favorite part because they jump up out of a deep sleep and are very scared. They expect to see a monster but it is only their friend.

21

Instant Independent Reading Response Activities Scholastic Professional Books

Favorite Part

Book Title: _____

This is a picture of my favorite part.

My favorite part of the book was _____

_____

_____

This was my favorite part because _____

_____

_____

_____

Name _____ Date _____

PROJECT 3
Bookmark

Materials

- ✔ your book
- ✔ Bookmark sheet
- ✔ crayons or markers
- ✔ pencil
- ✔ scissors
- ✔ 8½-inch by 3-inch piece of heavy paper
- ✔ hole punch
- ✔ 10-inch piece of yarn

Steps:

1. On the front of the bookmark, draw a picture that represents the book.

2. On the back, fill in the information about your book.

3. Cut out the front and back of the bookmark.

4. Glue the front of the bookmark onto the heavy paper. Glue the back of the bookmark onto the other side.

5. Punch a hole through the circle at the top of the bookmark.

6. Thread the yarn through the hole and tie a knot.

Bookmark Example

Name _____ Date _____

Book Title: The Kidnapped King

This book is about a kidnapping! The king, queen, and prince have been kidnapped. Dink, Josh, and Ruth Rose help solve the mystery.

Instant Independent Reading Response Activities Scholastic Professional Books

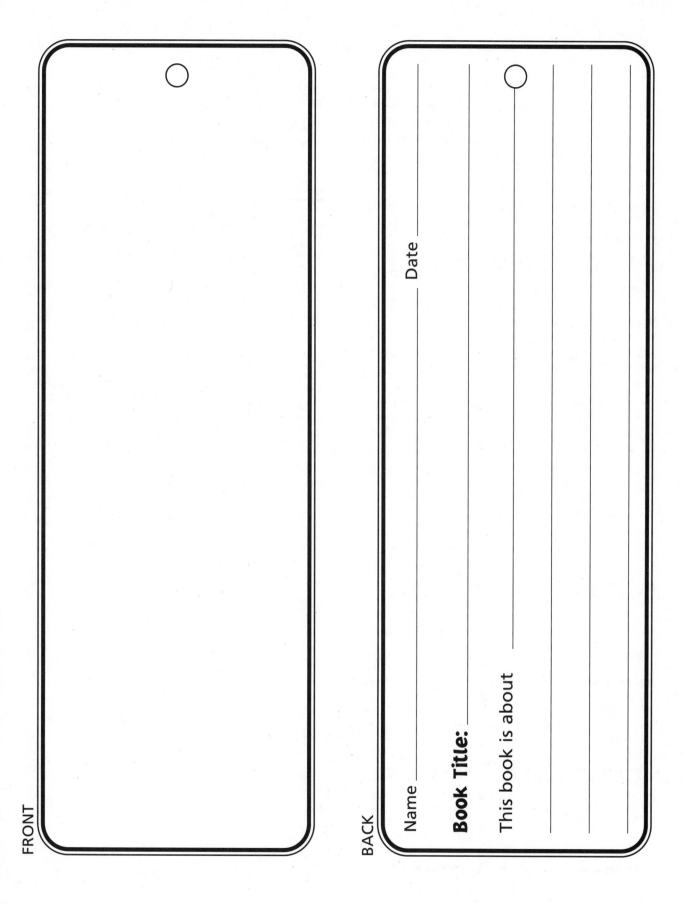

FRONT

BACK

Name _____

Date _____

Book Title: _____

This book is about _____

Name _____ Date _____

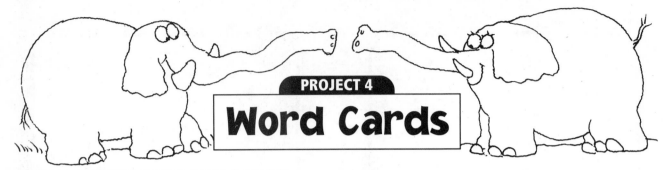

Word Cards

Materials

✔ your book

✔ Word Cards sheet

✔ pencil

✔ scissors

Steps:

1. Look through your book. Choose four words that you do not know.

2. Write one word on each card.

3. Write a sentence using each word.

4. Cut out the cards.

5. Write your name on the back of the cards.

6. Share your words with a partner.

Word Cards Example

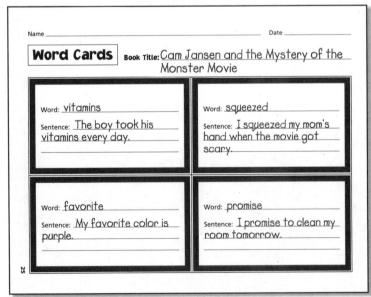

Instant Independent Reading Response Activities   Scholastic Professional Books

Instant Independent Reading Response Activities Scholastic Professional Books

Name _____

Date _____

Word Cards | Book Title: _____

Word: _____

Sentence: _____

Word: _____

Sentence: _____

Word: _____

Sentence: _____

Word: _____

Sentence: _____

Name _____ Date _____

PROJECT 5

Picture Mural

Materials

- ✔ your book
- ✔ Picture Mural sheet
- ✔ pencil
- ✔ old magazines, scissors, and glue (or crayons or markers)

Steps:

1. In the middle of the Picture Mural sheet, write the topic of your book.

2. Look through magazines for pictures that relate to the topic of your book. Cut out four pictures that relate to the topic. (If you can't find pictures in a magazine, draw four pictures instead.)

3. Glue one picture in each box.

4. On the line, write a label for each picture.

Picture Mural Example

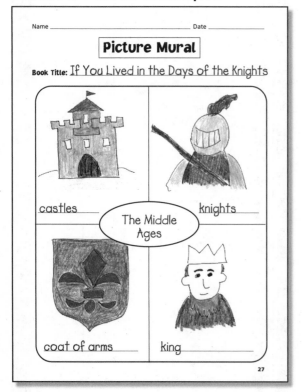

Instant Independent Reading Response Activities   Scholastic Professional Books

Name _____ Date _____

Picture Mural

Book Title: _____

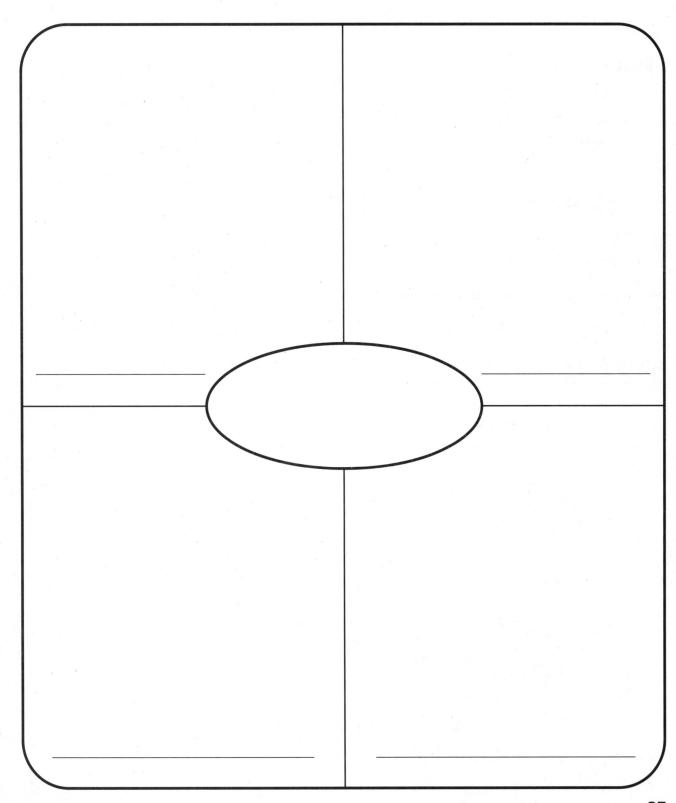

Instant Independent Reading Response Activities   Scholastic Professional Books

Name _____ Date _____

PROJECT 6

Word Graph

Materials

✔ your book

✔ Word Graph sheet

✔ pencil

Steps:

1. Pick four words from your book.

2. Write the words in the spaces at the bottom of the graph.

3. Each time the word appears in your book, write an **X** above that word. (If your book is short, look through the whole book. If your book is long, look through one chapter or a few pages.)

4. At the bottom of the sheet, write the word you found most often and the word you found least often.

Word Graph Example

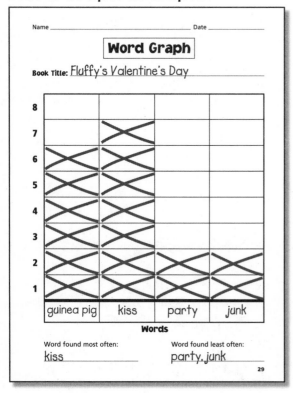

Name _____ Date _____

Word Graph

Book Title: Fluffy's Valentine's Day

	guinea pig	kiss	party	junk

Words

Word found most often:
kiss

Word found least often:
party, junk

29

28

Instant Independent Reading Response Activities   Scholastic Professional Books

Name _____ Date _____

Word Graph

Book Title: _____

8			
7			
6			
5			
4			
3			
2			
1			

Words

Word found most often: Word found least often:

_____   _____

Name _____ Date _____

PROJECT 7
Make a Web

Materials
✔ your book
✔ Make a Web sheet
✔ pencil
✔ crayons or markers

Steps:

1. In the middle of the web, write the topic of the book.

2. On each of the five lines, write one thing in the book that relates to the topic.

3. Draw a picture for each.

Make a Web Example

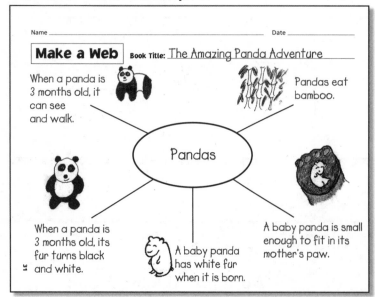

Instant Independent Reading Response Activities   Scholastic Professional Books

Instant Independent Reading Response Activities   Scholastic Professional Books

Name _____   Date _____

Make a Web

Book Title: _____

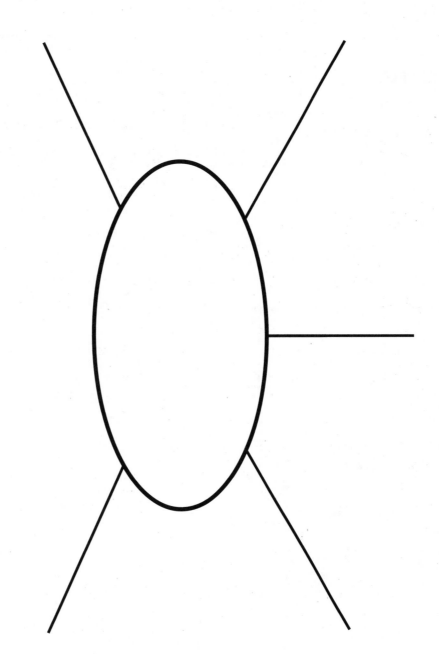

Name _____ Date _____

Create a New Page

Materials
✔ your book
✔ plain white paper
✔ crayons or markers
✔ pencil

Steps:

1. Think of an idea for a new page that you could add to your book.

2. Draw a picture of the new page.

3. Write a few sentences about what is happening in the picture. Try to write in the style of the author.

Create a New Page Example

Good Work, Amelia Bedelia

Mrs. Rogers asked Amelia Bedelia to draw the drapes. Amelia draws pictures on the drapes instead!

Instant Independent Reading Response Activities   Scholastic Professional Books

Name _____ Date _____

Story Sequence

Materials

✔ your book
✔ 5 index cards
✔ crayons or markers
✔ pencil
✔ glue or tape
✔ 2-inch by 24-inch
   paper strip

Steps:

1. On one index card, write the title and author.

2. Choose four key events from your book.

3. On each of the remaining index cards, draw a picture of one event.

4. Write a label for each picture.

5. Arrange the cards in the order the events happened. (Put the title card at the top and the first event card directly beow it.)

6. Glue or tape the index cards onto the paper strip.

7. Use the story sequence cards to help retell the story to another student.

Lon Po Po:
A Red Riding Hood
Story From China

by Ed Young

Story Sequence Example

The mother leaves to visit the grandmother. Shang, Tao, and Paotze are alone in the house.

A wolf pretends to be their grandmother coming for a visit and the children let him in.

Shang realizes he's a wolf and takes the other children into a gingko tree.

The children trick the wolf. He gets in a basket and they let him go.

Name _____ Date _____

PROJECT 10
Opposites

Materials

✔ your book

✔ Opposites sheet

✔ pencil

✔ crayons or markers

Steps:

1. Look in your book for four words that are opposites. (Examples: *up* and *down*, *large* and *small*)

2. Write each word in a box.

3. Draw a picture to show what each word means.

4. Share your opposites with another student.

Opposites Example

Instant Independent Reading Response Activities   Scholastic Professional Books

Name _____ Date _____

Opposites

Book Title: _____

Name _____ Date _____

PROJECT 11
Likes/Dislikes

Materials

✔ your book

✔ Likes/Dislikes sheet

✔ pencil

✔ crayons or markers

Steps:

1. Write two things in your book that you like.

2. Draw a picture of each.

3. Write two things in your book that you dislike.

4. Draw a picture of each.

5. Share your sheet with another student.

Likes/Dislikes Example

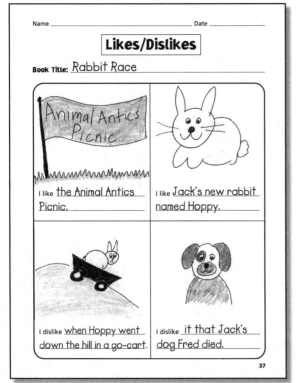

Instant Independent Reading Response Activities   Scholastic Professional Books

Name _____ Date _____

Likes/Dislikes

Book Title: _____

I like _____ _____	I like _____ _____
I dislike _____ _____	I dislike _____ _____

Name _____ Date _____

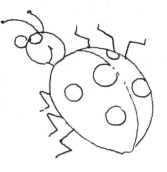

Make a Puzzle

Materials

✔ your book
✔ construction paper
✔ crayons or markers
✔ scissors
✔ small plastic bag

Steps:

1. At the top of the paper, write the title of the book.

2. Draw a picture of a scene from your book.

3. Cut apart your picture into puzzle pieces.

4. Put your pieces in the plastic bag.

5. Have a partner put together your puzzle.

Make a Puzzle Example

The Trumpet of the Swan

Instant Independent Reading Response Activities   Scholastic Professional Books

Name _____ Date _____

Scrambled Sentences

Materials

✔ your book

✔ two 2-inch by 18-inch paper strips, each a different color

✔ marker

✔ scissors

✔ 2 plastic bags

Steps:

1. Choose a sentence you like from your book.

2. With a marker, write the sentence on a paper strip.

3. Cut apart the paper strip between each word.

4. Shuffle the words and then arrange them in order without looking at the sentence in the book.

5. Shuffle the words again and then put them in a plastic bag.

6. Have a partner try to arrange the words in order.

7. Repeat steps 1–6 with a different sentence.

Scrambled Sentences Example

from *George's Marvelous Medicine* by Roald Dahl

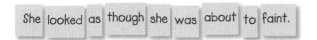

Name _____ Date _____

Paper-Bag Puppet

Materials

✔ your book
✔ white construction paper
✔ crayons or markers
✔ scissors
✔ glue
✔ small paper bag

Steps:

1. Choose a character from the book.

2. On the paper, draw the character's head. You may also choose to draw the character's arms and legs, as well as anything the character might hold or wear.

3. Color and cut out your pieces.

4. Glue them onto the bag.

5. Put your hand inside the bag and move the puppet to make it talk.

6. Have your puppet introduce the book to another student.

Paper-Bag Puppet Example

from *Mrs. Piggle-Wiggle*
by Betty MacDonald

PROJECT 15
Paper-Plate Puppet

Materials

✔ your book
✔ white construction paper
✔ crayons or markers
✔ scissors
✔ glue
✔ paper plate
✔ craft stick

Steps:

1. Choose a character from the book.

2. On the paper, draw the character's head. You may also choose to draw the character's arms and legs, as well as anything the character might hold or wear.

3. Color and cut out your pieces.

4. Glue them onto the front of the paper plate.

5. Glue the craft stick to the back of the plate.

6. Tell another student three things about your puppet.

Paper-Plate Puppet Example
from *Nate the Great*
by Marjorie Weinman Sharmat

Name _____ Date _____

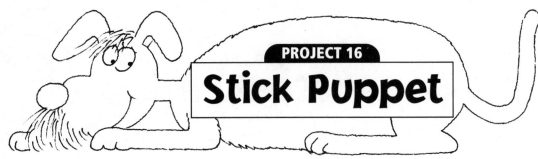

PROJECT 16
Stick Puppet

Materials

✔ your book
✔ white construction paper
✔ crayons or markers
✔ scissors
✔ glue
✔ craft stick

Steps:

1. Choose a character from the book.

2. On the paper, draw the character.

3. Color and cut out your drawing.

4. Glue the drawing onto the craft stick.

5. Invite another student to ask your puppet three questions about the book. Have the puppet answer the questions.

Stick Puppet Example
from *Stuart Little* by E. B. White

Instant Independent Reading Response Activities   Scholastic Professional Books

Name _____ Date _____

Advertise-a-Book Poster

Materials

✔ your book

✔ scrap paper

✔ pencil

✔ crayons or markers

✔ large sheet of construction paper

Advertise-a-Book Poster Example

Who Stole the Wizard of Oz?
by Avi

Go on an adventure with Becky and Tom as they try to solve a mystery! They must put together a treasure map before the thief does. Follow the clues to...

the Checkerboard Library

the apartment building

the Railroad Hotel

Steps:

1. Think about what pictures and words you could put on a poster to advertise your book. Draw a sketch of your poster on scrap paper. (Make sure not to tell the ending of the book.) Include the following on your poster:

   • book title

   • author

   • a sentence or two that would make others want to read the book

   • three pictures that show interesting parts of the book

2. Draw your poster on construction paper.

3. Share your poster with another student. Ask the student what parts of the poster make the book seem interesting.

Name _____ Date _____

Sentence Sequence Chart

Materials

✔ your book
✔ Sentence Sequence Chart sheet
✔ pencil
✔ crayons or markers

Steps:

1. Look in your book for a sentence about the main character.

2. In the first box, write the character's name.

3. In the second box, write what the character did in the sentence.

4. In the third box, write the rest of the sentence.

5. In each box, draw a picture that illustrates what you wrote.

6. Share your sentence with another student.

Sentence Sequence Chart Example

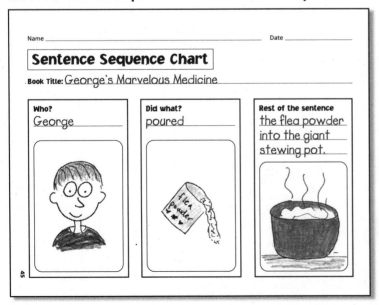

Instant Independent Reading Response Activities   Scholastic Professional Books

Instant Independent Reading Response Activities   Scholastic Professional Books

Name _____   Date _____

Sentence Sequence Chart

Book Title: _____

Who?

Did what?

Rest of the sentence

Name _____ Date _____

PROJECT 19
Story Flip Book

Materials
✔ your book
✔ Story Flip Book sheet
✔ scissors
✔ crayons or markers
✔ pencil

Steps:

1. Fold the sheet along the dotted line.

2. Cut the sheet along the dark solid lines.

3. Under the Main Character flap, draw a picture of the main character. Write the character's name below the picture.

4. Under the Problem flap, draw the problem in the story. Write a sentence describing the problem.

5. Under the Solution flap, draw the solution to the problem. Write a sentence explaining the solution.

6. On the back of the story flip book, write your name and the title of the book.

Story Flip Book Example

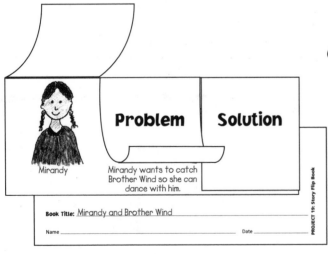

Mirandy

Problem   **Solution**

Mirandy wants to catch Brother Wind so she can dance with him.

Book Title: Mirandy and Brother Wind

Name _____   Date _____

PROJECT 19: Story Flip Book

Instant Independent Reading Response Activities   Scholastic Professional Books

Name _____ Date _____

Book Title: _____

Solution

Problem

Main Character

PROJECT 19: Story Flip Book

Name _____ Date _____

Character Map

Materials

✔ your book
✔ Character Map sheet
✔ pencil
✔ crayons or markers

Steps:

1. Choose a character from your book.

2. In the circle, write the character's name.

3. In box 1, draw a picture showing how the character feels at one point in the book. Write a sentence about it.

4. In box 2, draw picture of something the character likes. Write a sentence about it.

5. In box 3, draw a picture of something the character does in the story. Write a sentence about it.

6. In box 4, tell whether the character seems real to you. Tell why.

Character Map Example

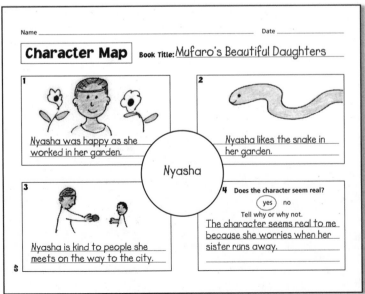

Instant Independent Reading Response Activities   Scholastic Professional Books

Name _____

Date _____

Character Map

Book Title: _____

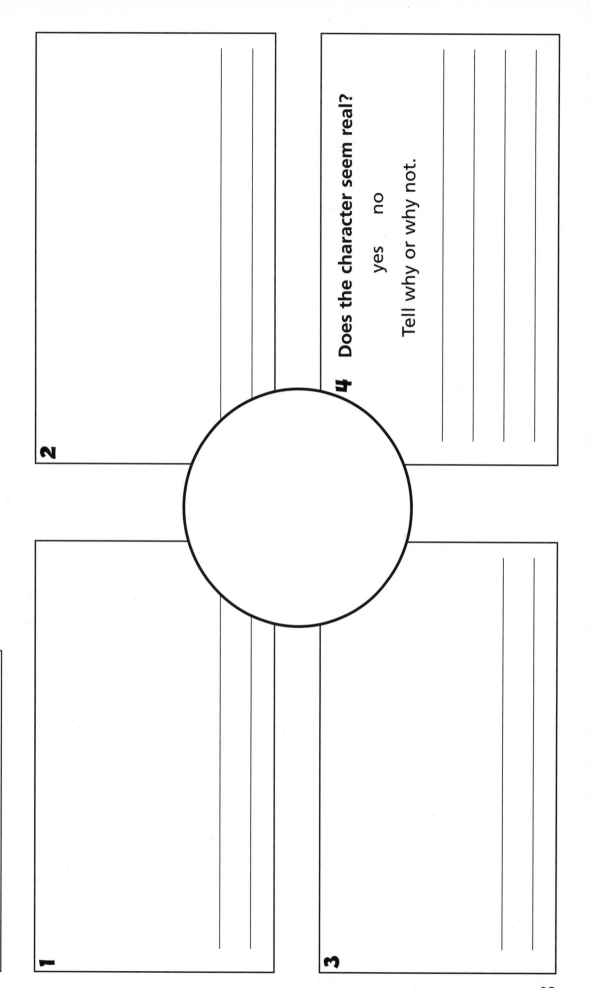

2

1

3

4 Does the character seem real?

yes   no

Tell why or why not.

Name _____ Date _____

Book Award

Materials

✔ your book

✔ Book Award sheet

✔ pencil

✔ crayons or markers

✔ scissors

Steps:

1. Think about what kind of award you want to give your book. Here are some examples:

- best characters
- best story
- best illustrations
- best ending
- best descriptions

2. At the top, write the kind of award you are giving the book.

3. Write why the book deserves the award and draw a picture.

4. Fill in the information at the bottom of the award.

5. Color the award.

6. Cut out the award.

Book Award Example

Award:
Best Story

This book deserves this award because the story is funny and has lots of action, like when the giant battles the dragon.

Book Title: Knights of the Kitchen Table
Author: Jon Scieszka

Award Given By: Alex

Date: December 2

Instant Independent Reading Response Activities   Scholastic Professional Books

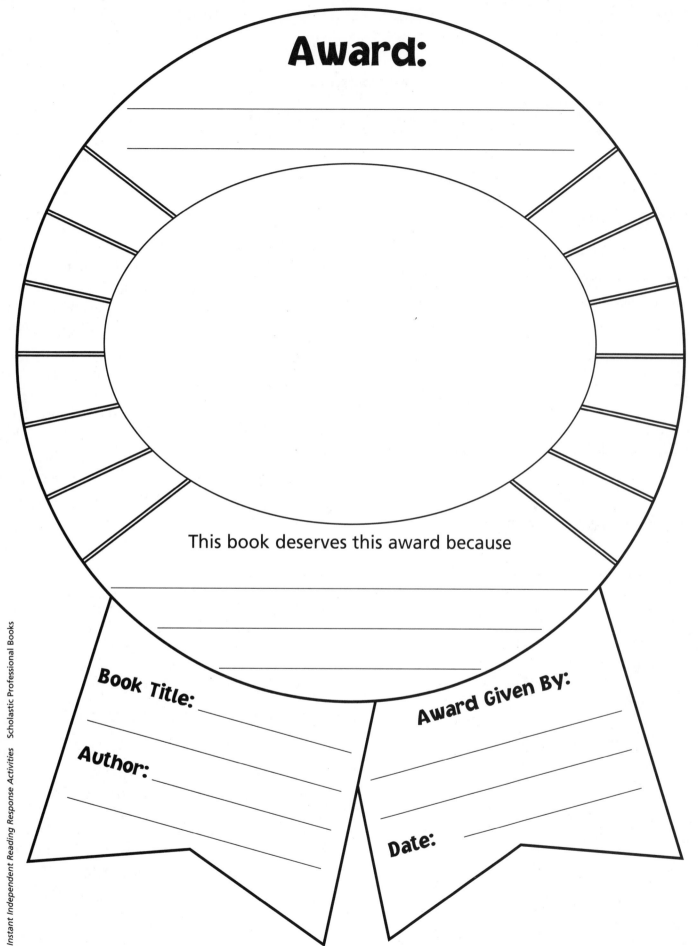

Award:

This book deserves this award because

Book Title: _____

Author: _____

Award Given By: _____

Date: _____

Name _____ Date _____

Adjective Fan

Materials

✔ your book

✔ plain white paper

✔ pencil or fine-tipped markers

Adjective Fan Example

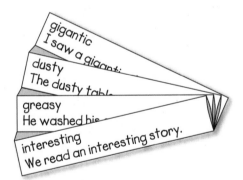

Steps:

1. Fold your paper like a fan. First fold about 1½ inches down from the top. Then turn your paper over and make another fold that is the same width. Continue in the same way until the entire paper is folded.

2. Unfold your paper and position it vertically. The folds in your paper will look like rows.

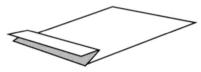

gigantic
I saw a gigantic ship.

lovely
Lovely flowers grow in the garden.

dusty
The dusty table was broken.

3. Look in your book for adjectives.

4. In the top row, write an adjective.

5. Beneath it, write a sentence that includes the adjective.

6. In the next row, write another adjective and use that adjective in a sentence.

7. Continue until your fan is full. If you want, fill in the other side of your fan.

Instant Independent Reading Response Activities Scholastic Professional Books

Name _____ Date _____

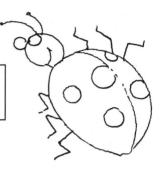

PROJECT 23
Story Questions

Materials
✔ your book
✔ 3 index cards
✔ pencil

Steps:

1. Think of three questions about your book.

2. Write one question on each of the index cards.

3. On the other side of the index cards, write the answers. Write your initials in the corner of each card.

4. Share your questions with another student who has read the same book. Ask the student to answer the questions.

Story Questions Example

FRONT

BACK

Who wrote the note to Song Lee?   M.C.

Mary wrote the note.

What book did Miss Mackle read?   M.C.

She read Lovable Lyle.

Whom did Harry tattle on?   M.C.

Harry tattled on Mary.

Name _____ Date _____

New Ending

Materials

✔ your book

✔ New Ending sheet

✔ pencil

✔ crayons or markers

Steps:

1. Think of a different ending for your book and write it down.

2. Draw a picture to illustrate your ending.

3. Share your ending with another student who has read the same book.

New Ending Example

Name _____ Date _____

New Ending

Book Title: The Littles Go Exploring

Author: John Peterson

Write a new ending for the book.

The Littles take their boat, the Discoverer, on another adventure. While riding in their boat, they were hit by a fish! The boat tipped and the Littles fell in the water. Will Little saved Grandpa Little from the fish that was heading their way. All the Littles made it safely to shore. They were able to get the boat onto land, and then they headed home.

Draw a picture to go with your new ending.

55

Instant Independent Reading Response Activities   Scholastic Professional Books

New Ending

Book Title: _____

Author: _____

Write a new ending for the book.

_____

_____

_____

_____

_____

Draw a picture to go with your new ending.

Name _____ Date _____

PROJECT 25
Story Chart

Materials

✔ your book

✔ Story Chart sheet

✔ pencil

✔ crayons or markers

Steps:

1. Write a sentence describing the setting.

2. List the main characters.

3. Draw pictures of the beginning, middle, and ending of the story. Write a sentence about each.

4. Circle the face that matches what you thought of the book, then tell why.

5. Share your story chart with another student who has read the same book.

Story Chart Example

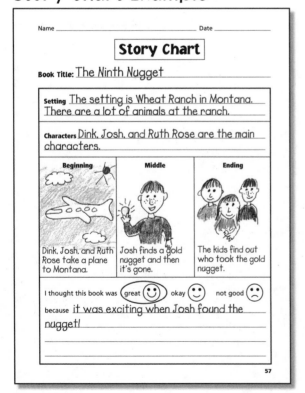

Instant Independent Reading Response Activities Scholastic Professional Books

Name _____ Date _____

Story Chart

Book Title: _____

Setting _____
_____
Characters _____
_____

Beginning	Middle	Ending

I thought this book was   great   okay   not good

because _____

_____

_____

Name _____ Date _____

Story Map

Materials

✔ your book

✔ Story Map sheet

✔ pencil

✔ crayons or markers

✔ scissors

Steps:

1. In the middle, write the title.

2. In the boxes, draw a picture to show each of the following:
- characters
- setting
- problem
- solution

3. Write a sentence about each.

4. Cut out the map.

Story Map Example

Instant Independent Reading Response Activities   Scholastic Professional Books

Name _____

Date _____

Story Map

Book Title: _____

Characters:

Setting:

Problem:

Solution:

Name _____ Date _____

Picture Walk

Materials
✔ your book
✔ Picture Walk sheet
✔ crayons or markers

Steps:

1. Write the title and author.

2. Think about how to retell the story in pictures.

3. Decide on three key events. They should retell the beginning, middle, and ending.

4. Draw a picture for each event in the order they happened.

Picture Walk Example

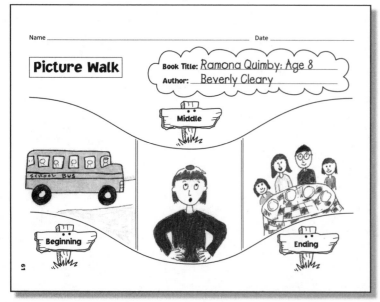

Instant Independent Reading Response Activities   Scholastic Professional Books

Name _____   Date _____

Picture Walk

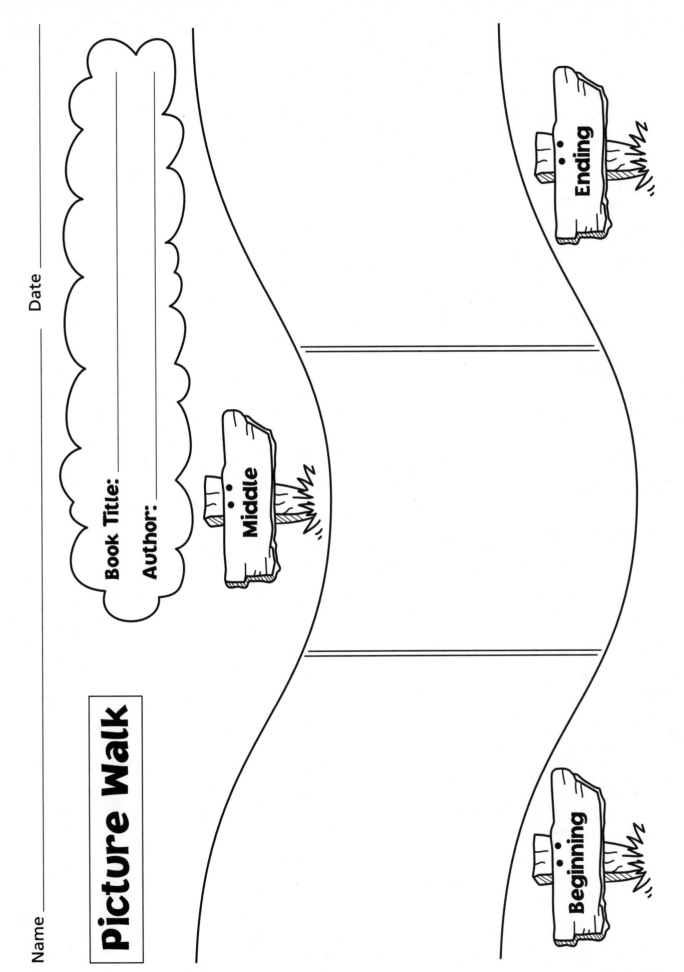

Book Title: _____

Author: _____

Beginning

Middle

Ending

Name _____ Date _____

Pyramid Diorama

Materials

✔ your book

✔ 3 Pyramid Diorama sheets

✔ scissors

✔ glue

✔ crayons or markers

✔ pencil

Steps:

1. Cut each sheet along the solid line at the bottom so that each sheet is a square.

2. Fold each square diagonally (corner to corner) along one dotted line. Open each square and fold it diagonally along the other line.

3. Cut along the solid line to the center, making two flaps.

4. On the uncut halves, draw pictures of the beginning, middle, and ending.

5. Label the sections *beginning*, *middle*, and *ending* and write a sentence for each.

6. Glue flap 1 on top of flap 2.

7. Glue the back sides of the three sections together.

Pyramid Diorama Example

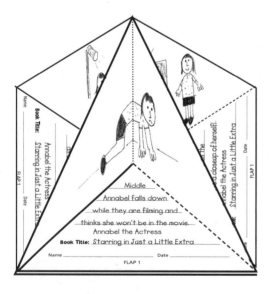

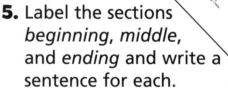

Instant Independent Reading Response Activities Scholastic Professional Books

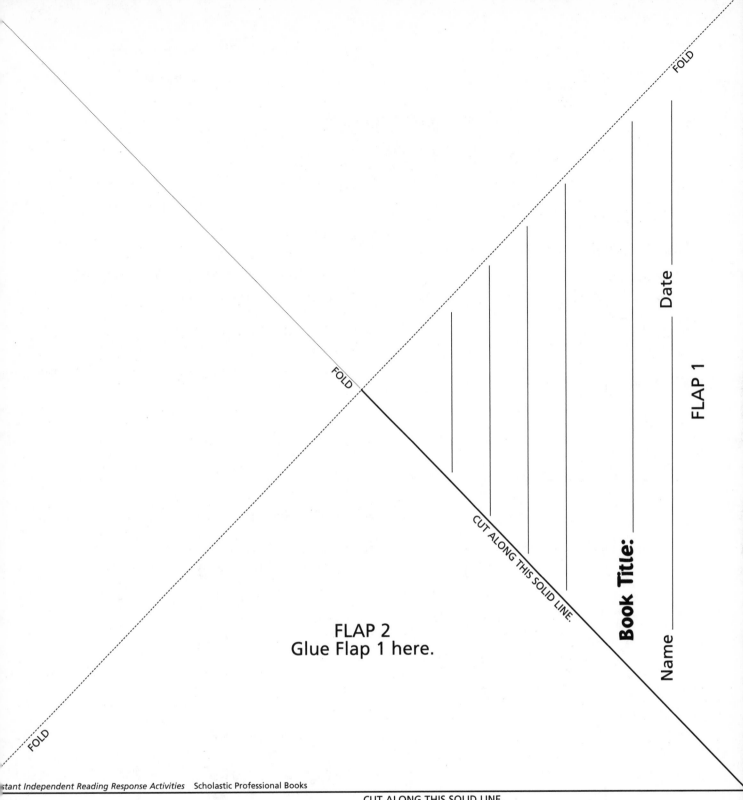

FOLD

FOLD

FLAP 1

Date

Book Title:

Name

CUT ALONG THIS SOLID LINE.

FOLD

FLAP 2
Glue Flap 1 here.

FOLD

stant Independent Reading Response Activities   Scholastic Professional Books

CUT ALONG THIS SOLID LINE.

PROJECT 28: Pyramid Diorama

63

Name _____ Date _____

PROJECT 29
Postcard

Materials

✔ your book

✔ Postcard sheet

✔ pencil

✔ scissors

✔ crayons or markers

Steps:

1. Fill in the information on the right side of the postcard.

2. On the lines, summarize the book. Write a sentence or two about each of the following:
  • characters
  • setting
  • problem
  • solution

3. Cut out the postcard.

4. Draw a stamp that shows something in the book. On the back, draw a picture of a scene from the book.

Postcard Example

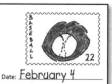

Book Title: In the Year of the Boar and Jackie Robinson
Author: Bette Bao Lord

Book Summary: Shirley and her parents move from China to New York. They are loyal to one another and help each other out. The problem in the story is that Shirley has a hard time getting used to her new home. The solution was for Shirley to be herself and make friends.

Date: February 4

To: Jamie Good
15 Boylston Str
Boston, MA

From: Marisa

Instant Independent Reading Response Activities Scholastic Professional Books

Book Title: _____

Author: _____

Book Summary: _____

Date: _____

To: _____

From: _____

Name _____ Date _____

PROJECT 30
Story Flag

Materials
✔ your book
✔ Story Flag sheet
✔ pencil
✔ crayons or markers
✔ scissors
✔ 2 straws or craft sticks
✔ tape or glue

Steps:

1. Write the title and author.

2. Write a sentence about the setting.

3. List the main characters.

4. Write a sentence telling your favorite part.

5. In the middle, draw a picture of your favorite part.

6. Color your picture.

7. Cut out the flag.

8. Attach two straws or craft sticks to the back of the flag along the edge of the paper. One straw or craft stick should extend below the paper so that you can hold it like a flag.

Story Flag Example

Book Title: Charlotte's Web
Author: E. B. White

Story Flag

SOME PIG

Setting: This book takes place in Mr. Zuckerman's barn where the animals live.

Characters: Fern, Wilbur, Charlotte, Templeton, Mr. and Mrs. Arable

Favorite Part: Charlotte writes a message in her web to save Wilbur.

Name _____ Date _____

Instant Independent Reading Response Activities   Scholastic Professional Books

Setting:_____

Story Flag

Book Title:_____

Author:_____

Characters:_____

Favorite Part:_____

Name _____

Date _____

Name _____ Date _____

Letter to the Author

Materials
✔ your book
✔ Letter to the Author sheet
✔ pencil
✔ crayons or markers

Steps:

1. Write a letter to the author. You might include the following in the letter:

- your favorite part of the book
- other things that you liked about the book
- questions about the book
- questions about the writing process

2. Draw a border around your letter that matches the theme of the book.

Letter to the Author Example

Name _____ Date _____

Letter to the Author

Book Title: _____

Dear Judy Blume, ,
　　　I liked your book Freckle Juice. My favorite part of the book is when Andrew drinks the freckle juice. I also liked the illustrations. I have one question about the book. What is the secret freckle remover that Miss Kelly gave to Andrew? Also, where did you get the idea for this book?
_____

Your friend,
Denzel

69

Instant Independent Reading Response Activities   Scholastic Professional Books

Name _____ Date _____

Letter to the Author

Book Title: _____

Dear _____,

_____

_____

_____

_____

_____

_____

_____

_____

_____

_____

_____

Name _____ Date _____

PROJECT 32
Story Cube

Materials

✔ your book
✔ Story Cube sheet
✔ pencil
✔ crayons or markers
✔ scissors
✔ glue or tape

Steps:

1. Fill in each numbered square as follows:

① Write the book title, author, and your name.

② Draw the main character.

③ Draw the main setting of the story.

④ Draw a picture to show the problem in the story.

⑤ Draw a picture to show the solution to the problem.

⑥ Draw your favorite part of the book.

2. Cut out the cube along the solid lines.

3. Fold along the dashed lines.

4. Glue or tape together to form a cube.

Story Cube Example

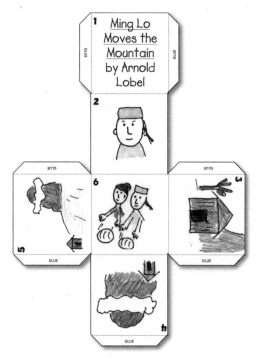

Instant Independent Reading Response Activities Scholastic Professional Books

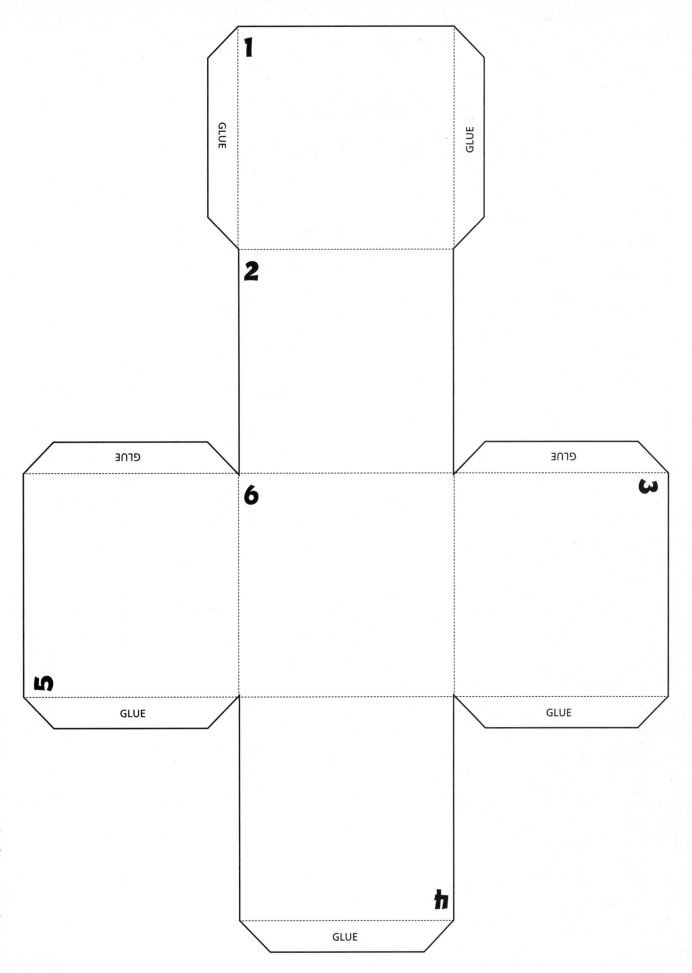

Name _____ Date _____

PROJECT 33
Character Feeling Chart

Materials
✔ your book
✔ Character Feeling Chart sheet
✔ pencil
✔ crayons or markers

Character Feeling Chart Example

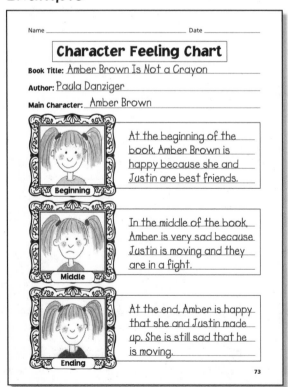

Name _____ Date _____

Character Feeling Chart

Book Title: Amber Brown Is Not a Crayon

Author: Paula Danziger

Main Character: Amber Brown

Beginning — At the beginning of the book, Amber Brown is happy because she and Justin are best friends.

Middle — In the middle of the book, Amber is very sad because Justin is moving and they are in a fight.

Ending — At the end, Amber is happy that she and Justin made up. She is still sad that he is moving.

73

Steps:

1. Write the title, author, and main character's name.

2. How does the main character feel at the beginning of the story? In the Beginning frame, draw the character's face to show how he or she feels.

3. Write a sentence to tell why the character feels this way.

4. In the Middle frame, draw the character's face to show how he or she feels in the middle of the story.

5. Write a sentence to tell why.

6. In the Ending frame, draw the character's face to show how he or she feels at the end of the story.

7. Write a sentence to tell why.

Instant Independent Reading Response Activities   Scholastic Professional Books

Name _____ Date _____

Character Feeling Chart

Book Title: _____

Author: _____

Main Character: _____

Beginning

_____
_____
_____

Middle

_____
_____
_____

Ending

_____
_____
_____

Name _____   Date _____

PROJECT 34
Mirror, Mirror

Materials
✔ your book
✔ Mirror, Mirror sheet
✔ crayons or markers
✔ pencil

Steps:

1. Draw a different character in each mirror.

2. Write a sentence or two about each character.

Mirror, Mirror Example

Instant Independent Reading Response Activities   Scholastic Professional Books

Name _____

Date _____

Mirror, Mirror

Book Title: _____

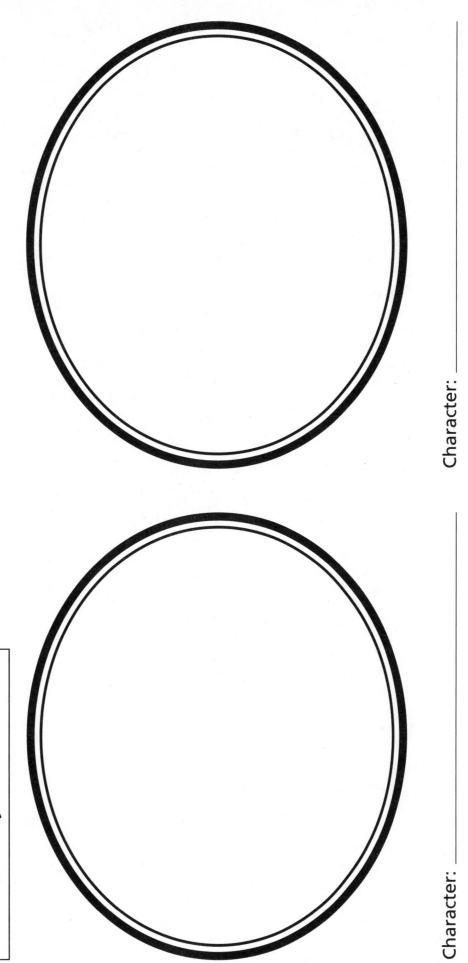

Character: _____

Character: _____

Name _____ Date _____

PROJECT 35
Noun Flip Book

Materials

✔ your book

✔ Noun Flip Book sheet

✔ scissors

✔ pencil

✔ crayons or markers

Steps:

1. Fold the paper along the dotted line.

2. Cut the paper along the heavy solid lines.

3. Under the Person flap, draw a picture of a character from your book. Write the character's name below the picture.

4. Under the Place flap, draw a picture of a place from your book. Write the name of the place below the picture.

5. Under the Thing flap, draw a picture of a thing from your book. Write the name of the thing below the picture.

6. On the back of the flip book, write your name and the title of the book.

Noun Flip Book Example

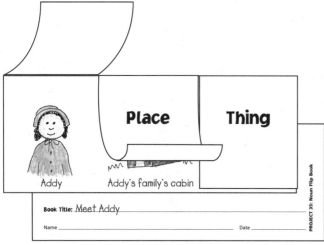

Instant Independent Reading Response Activities   Scholastic Professional Books

Thing

Place

Person

PROJECT 36
Rhyming Chain

Materials

✔ your book
✔ Rhyming Chain sheet
✔ pencil
✔ scissors
✔ glue or tape

Rhyming Chain Example

Steps:

1. Choose a word from your book that you can rhyme with other words.

2. Write the word in the box at the top of the page.

3. In each of the other boxes, write a different word that rhymes with the word in the top box.

4. Cut along the lines.

5. Glue or tape the ends of one strip together.

6. Link this circle with another strip to start a chain. Tape the ends of that strip together.

7. Continue linking strips together to form a chain.

8. Write your name, date, and the book title. Add this link to the chain.

Instant Independent Reading Response Activities Scholastic Professional Books

Name _____ Date _____

Book Title: _____

Word from book:

PROJECT 36: Rhyming Chain

Name _____ Date _____

Real or Make-Believe?

Materials

- ✔ your book
- ✔ Real or Make-Believe? sheet
- ✔ pencil
- ✔ crayons or markers

Steps:

1. In the Real column, list four things from your book that could really exist or happen.

2. In the box, draw a picture of one thing on this list.

3. In the Make-Believe column, list four things from your book that could not really exist or happen.

4. In the box, draw a picture of one thing on this list.

Real or Make Believe? Example

Name _____ Date _____

Real or Make-Believe?

Book Title: Frog and Toad Are Friends

Real	Make-Believe
1. Frogs and toads live near water.	1. Frogs and toads do not live in houses.
2. Frogs and toads may hibernate in winter.	2. Toads do not sleep in beds.
3. Frogs swim in water.	3. Frogs do not wear bathing suits.
4. Frogs and toads are green.	4. Frogs and toads do not send letters.

81

Name _____ Date _____

Real or Make-Believe?

Book Title: _____

Real	Make-Believe
1. _____ _____	1. _____ _____
2. _____ _____	2. _____ _____
3. _____ _____	3. _____ _____
4. _____ _____	4. _____ _____

Name _____ Date _____

Character Venn Diagram

Materials

✔ your book

✔ Character Venn Diagram sheet

✔ pencil

Steps:

1. Choose a character from the book. You will compare yourself to this character. Write the character's name on the line in the right circle.

2. Write your name in the left circle.

3. In the middle section, write what you and the character have in common.

4. In your circle, write things that describe you but not the character.

5. In the character's circle, write things that describe the character but not you.

Character Venn Diagram Example

Name _____ Date _____

Character Venn Diagram

Book Title: The Summer of the Swans

Lila
(your name)

Both

Charlie
(character's name)

am 11 years old
live in a city
am a girl

like birds
have an older sister
have gotten lost

is 10 years old
lives in the country
is a boy

83

Instant Independent Reading Response Activities   Scholastic Professional Books

Instant Independent Reading Response Activities   Scholastic Professional Books

Name _____   Date _____

Character Venn Diagram

Book Title: _____

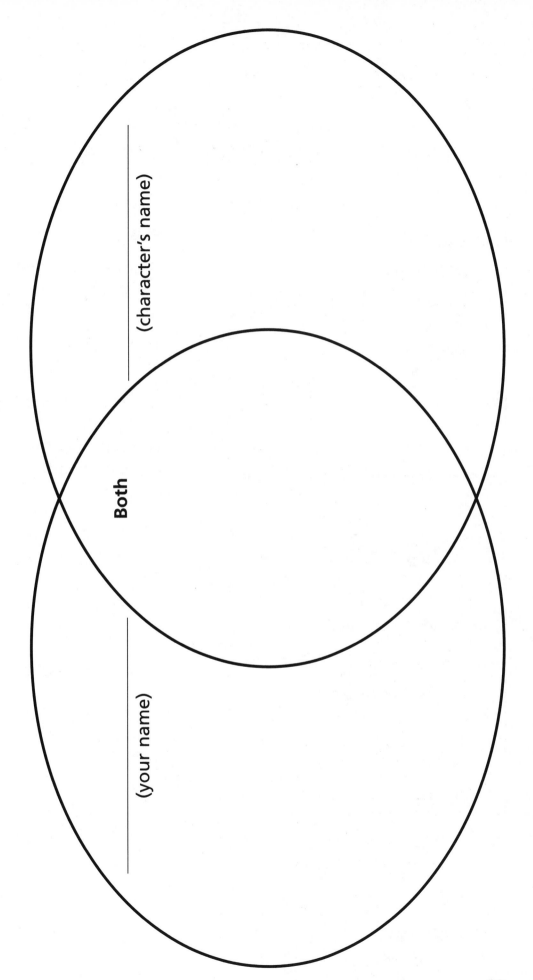

(character's name)

Both

(your name)

Name _____ Date _____

PROJECT 39
Fact Finder

Materials
✔ your book
✔ Fact Finder sheet
✔ pencil

Steps:

1. At the top of the ladder, write the topic of your book.

2. On each of the five rungs, list one fact from your book. Be sure to write in complete sentences.

3. Draw a star by the fact that you think is the most important. On the back of the paper, explain why it is important.

Fact Finder Example

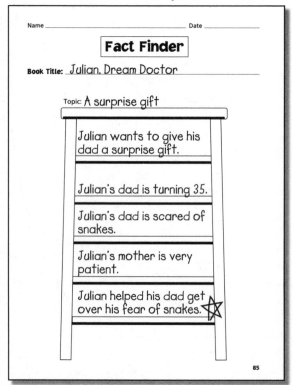

Instant Independent Reading Response Activities Scholastic Professional Books

Name _____ Date _____

Fact Finder

Book Title: _____

Topic:

Name _____ Date _____

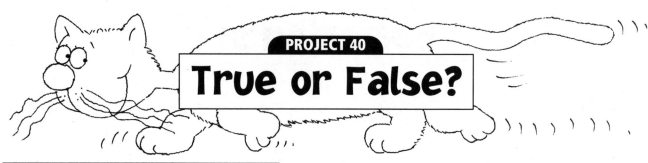

PROJECT 40
True or False?

Materials
✔ your book
✔ True or False? sheet
✔ pencil
✔ crayons or markers

Steps:

1. List three statements about your book that are true.

2. Draw a picture to illustrate one true statement.

3. List three statements about your book that are false.

4. Draw a picture to illustrate one false statement.

True or False? Example

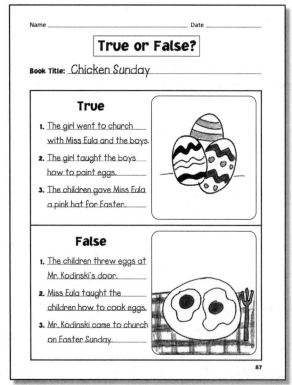

Instant Independent Reading Response Activities Scholastic Professional Books

True or False?

Book Title: _____

True

1. _____

_____

2. _____

_____

3. _____

_____

False

1. _____

_____

2. _____

_____

3. _____

_____

Instant Independent Reading Response Activities   Scholastic Professional Books

Name _____ Date _____

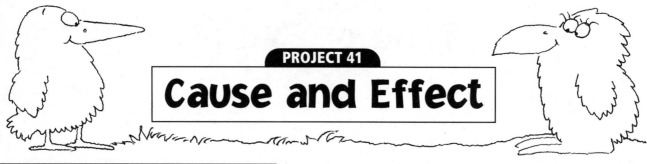

Cause and Effect

Materials

✔ your book

✔ Cause and Effect sheet

  (you may need more than one sheet)

✔ pencil

✔ scissors

✔ glue

✔ large sheet of construction paper

Steps:

1. In one arrow, write something that happens in the book. (This is the *cause*.)

2. In the box beside the arrow, write what happens as a result. (This is the *effect*.)

3. Try to fill in several different cause and effect sheets.

4. Cut out the arrows and boxes.

5. Position the construction paper vertically.

6. Glue the arrows and boxes onto the paper from top to bottom in the order they happen in the book.

7. Write the title and author on the construction paper.

Cause and Effect Example

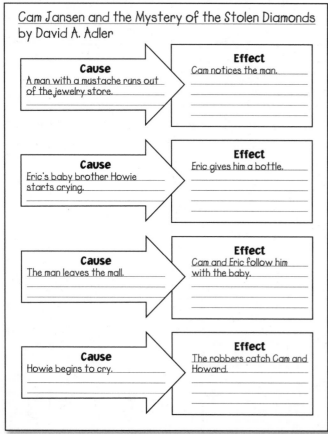

Cam Jansen and the Mystery of the Stolen Diamonds
by David A. Adler

Cause
A man with a mustache runs out of the jewelry store.

Effect
Cam notices the man.

Cause
Eric's baby brother Howie starts crying.

Effect
Eric gives him a bottle.

Cause
The man leaves the mall.

Effect
Cam and Eric follow him with the baby.

Cause
Howie begins to cry.

Effect
The robbers catch Cam and Howard.

Instant Independent Reading Response Activities   Scholastic Professional Books

Name _____

Date _____

Cause and Effect

Book Title: _____

Effect

Cause

Effect

Cause

Name _____ Date _____

PROJECT 42

Just the Facts

Materials

✔ your book

✔ Just the Facts sheet

✔ pencil

Steps:

1. Think about facts in your book. Write the most important fact in the oval.

2. Write five other facts on the lines.

3. Write the book title.

Just the Facts Example

Name _____ Date _____

Just the Facts

Book Title: _A Girl Named Helen Keller_

Facts

1. Helen Keller could not see or hear.

2. At first, Helen often misbehaved.

3. Helen's parents hired Anne Sullivan to teach Helen.

4. Anne taught Helen to finger spell.

5. Helen went to school and met many people.

Important Fact

Helen Keller spent her life helping blind and deaf people.

91

Instant Independent Reading Response Activities   Scholastic Professional Books

Name _____ Date _____

Just the Facts

Book Title: _____

Facts

1. _____

2. _____

3. _____

4. _____

5. _____

Important Fact

Name _____ Date _____

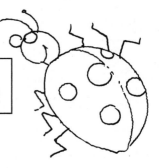

PROJECT 43

Facts and Opinions

Materials
✔ your book
✔ Facts and Opinions sheet
✔ pencil

Steps:

1. In the Facts column, write five facts about your book. Be sure to write in complete sentences.

2. In the Opinions column, write five opinions. Try to make each opinion about the same topic as the fact beside it.

Facts and Opinions Example

Name _____ Date _____

Facts and Opinions

Book Title: Sarah, Plain and Tall

Facts	Opinions
1. Clover is a prairie flower.	1. Clover is the prettiest flower.
2. A squall is noisy storm with hail and lightning.	2. Squalls are scary.
3. Anna's mother died after Caleb was born.	3. Babies make everyone happy.
4. Scallops leave behind their shells.	4. Scallops are delicious.
5. The sea is salty.	5. The sea is more fun than a lake.

93

Instant Independent Reading Response Activities   Scholastic Professional Books

Name _____ Date _____

Facts and Opinions

Book Title: _____

Facts	Opinions
1. _____ _____	1. _____ _____
2. _____ _____	2. _____ _____
3. _____ _____	3. _____ _____
4. _____ _____	4. _____ _____
5. _____ _____	5. _____ _____

Name _____ Date _____

Event Timeline

Materials

✔ your book

✔ Event Timeline sheet

✔ pencil

✔ crayons or markers

Steps:

1. Think about the important events that take place in your book.

2. Write these events in the order they happen. Start at the top of the page.

3. Along the left side of the page, write when these events happened. For example, what time of day or season was it? If you are not sure, label the left side *beginning, middle,* and *ending*.

4. If you have space, add some small pictures to illustrate the events on the timeline.

Event Timeline Example

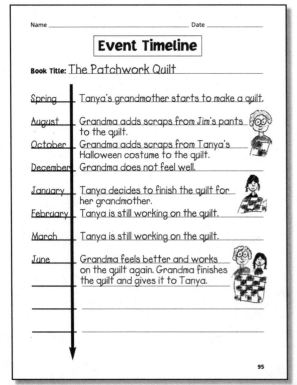

Name _____ Date _____

Event Timeline

Book Title: The Patchwork Quilt _____

Spring	Tanya's grandmother starts to make a quilt.
August	Grandma adds scraps from Jim's pants to the quilt.
October	Grandma adds scraps from Tanya's Halloween costume to the quilt.
December	Grandma does not feel well.
January	Tanya decides to finish the quilt for her grandmother.
February	Tanya is still working on the quilt.
March	Tanya is still working on the quilt.
June	Grandma feels better and works on the quilt again. Grandma finishes the quilt and gives it to Tanya.

95

Instant Independent Reading Response Activities Scholastic Professional Books

Name _____ Date _____

Event Timeline

Book Title: _____

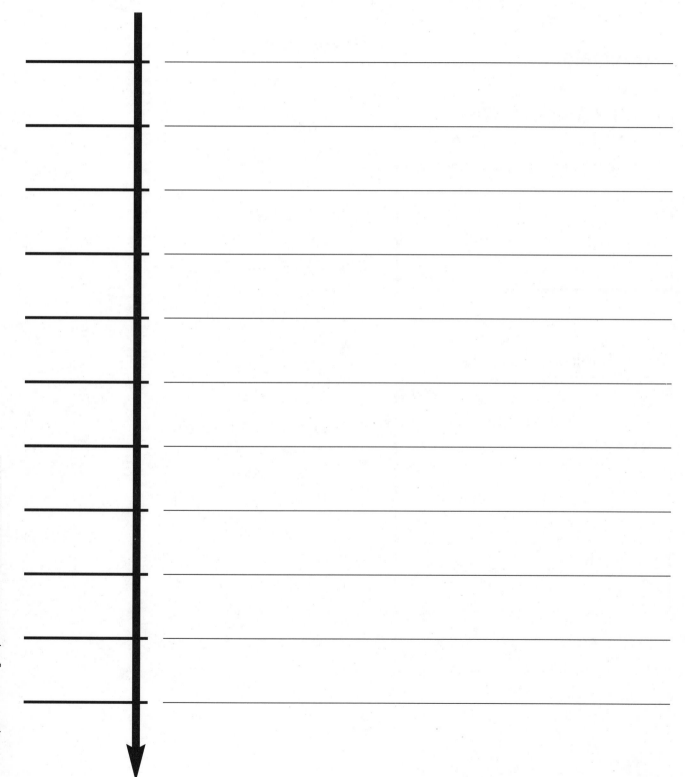

Name _____ Date _____

PROJECT 45
Story Booklet

Materials
✔ your book
✔ Story Booklet Forms 1, 2, and 3 (Note to Teacher: Make double-sided copies of Forms 1, 2, and 3 as they appear in the book.)
✔ stapler
✔ pencil
✔ crayons or marker

Steps:

1. Fold each form on the dashed line.

2. Place form 2 inside form 1.

3. Place form 3 inside form 2.

4. Staple the forms together along the fold.

5. Fill in the information on each page.

6. Draw a picture to illustrate the information on each page.

Story Booklet Example

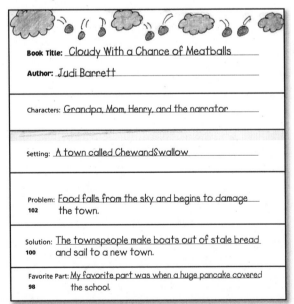

Book Title: Cloudy With a Chance of Meatballs

Author: Judi Barrett

Characters: Grandpa, Mom, Henry, and the narrator

Setting: A town called ChewandSwallow

Problem: Food falls from the sky and begins to damage
102 the town.

Solution: The townspeople make boats out of stale bread
100 and sail to a new town.

Favorite Part: My favorite part was when a huge pancake covered
98 the school.

Instant Independent Reading Response Activities   Scholastic Professional Books

Author: _____

Book Title: _____

Story Booklet
Form 1

Instant Independent Reading Response Activities Scholastic Professional Books

Name _____ Date _____

Favorite Part: _____

Instant Independent Reading Response Activities   Scholastic Professional Books

**Story Booklet
Form 2**

Name _____ Date _____

Solution: _____

Instant Independent Reading Response Activities   Scholastic Professional Books

Story Booklet
Form 3

Name _____ Date _____

Problem: _____

Instant Independent Reading Response Activities   Scholastic Professional Books

Name _____ Date _____

PROJECT 46
Setting Map

Materials

✔ your book

✔ plain white paper

✔ pencil

✔ crayons or markers

✔ 2 index cards

Steps:

1. Think about all the different places in the book.

2. Using a pencil, draw a map of the most important places on a sheet of paper.

3. Write labels of the places on your map.

4. Color your map.

5. On each index card, write a question that you could ask another student about your map.

6. Share your map with a classmate. Ask your classmate to use the map to answer the questions.

Setting Map Example

Name _____ Date _____

PROJECT 47
Story Quilt Square

Materials

✔ your book

✔ Story Quilt Square sheet

✔ pencil

✔ crayons or markers

Steps:

1. In the middle square, write the book title and author. Draw a picture about the book.

2. In each of the four corners, draw a picture that represents an important object or character from the book. Label your pictures.

3. Add stitches around the center square with a crayon or marker.

Story Quilt Square Example

Instant Independent Reading Response Activities   Scholastic Professional Books

Name _____ Date _____

Story Quilt Square

Book Title:

_____

_____

Author: _____

Name _____ Date _____

Book Banner

Materials

✔ your book
✔ Book Banner sheet
✔ scissors
✔ 12-inch piece of yarn
✔ glue
✔ pencil
✔ crayons or markers

Steps:

1. Cut out the banner along the dark black lines.

2. Fold the top of the banner back on the dotted line.

3. Place the yarn beneath the banner fold so that a few inches of yarn stick out on each side.

4. Glue the flap to the back of the banner.

5. On the banner, include the following:
   • title
   • author
   • a picture that represents the theme of the book
   • one or two sentences describing an important idea or lesson that the book teaches

6. Display your banner.

Book Banner Example

Book Title: How My Parents Learned to Eat

Author: Ina R. Friedman

Different people from different places can teach one another their ways. This helps people understand and respect one another.

Instant Independent Reading Response Activities Scholastic Professional Books

Book Banner

Book Title: _____

Author: _____

_____

_____

_____

PROJECT 49

Create a Poem

Materials

✔ your book

✔ Create a Poem sheet

✔ pencil

✔ crayons or markers

Steps:

1. Choose a person, place, or thing from your book for the subject of a poem.

2. Fill in the first blank on each line with the subject of the poem.

3. Fill in the second blank on each line with words that describe the subject.

4. Draw a picture to illustrate your poem.

Create a Poem Example

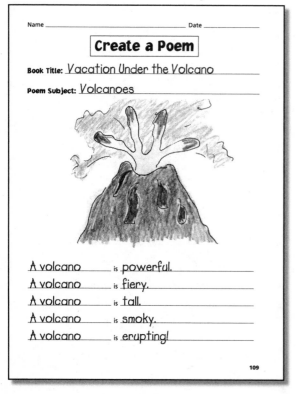

Name _____ Date _____

Create a Poem

Book Title: _____

Poem Subject: _____

_____ is _____

_____ is _____

_____ is _____

_____ is _____

_____ is _____

Name _____ Date _____

PROJECT 50
Book News

Materials

✔ your book

✔ Book News sheet

✔ pencil

✔ crayons or markers

Steps:

1. Write the title and author.

2. In the box, draw a picture of the most exciting part of the book.

3. Write a caption under the picture. The caption is a short sentence that tells about the picture.

4. Imagine that you are a news reporter. Write a short article about the exciting part of your book. In your article, answer these questions:
  • Who?
  • What?
  • Where?
  • When?
  • Why?

5. Give your article a title.

Book News Example

Name _____ Date _____

BOOK NEWS

Book Title: The Adventures of Spider

Author: Joyce Cooper Arkhurst

Spider Gets Thin Waist!
(article title)

Yesterday, on the day of the harvest festival, Spider changed his shape! He used to be round, but now he has a thin waist. Here is how it happened. Spider could not decide which village's festival would have the most food. He stood in the middle of two villages and tied a long rope around his waist. His son Kuma took one end of the rope to one village. His other son Kwaku took the other end of the rope to a different village. They were supposed to pull the rope when the food was ready, so Spider could eat at both festivals. But the food was ready at the same time. When the sons pulled the rope, Spider's waist got thin. From now on, all spiders will have a new shape.

Spider prepares for the festivals by tying a rope around his waist.
(caption)

111

Instant Independent Reading Response Activities Scholastic Professional Books

Name ______________________________ Date ______________

BOOK NEWS

Book Title: ______________________________

Author: ______________________________

____

(article title)

(caption)

Notes